# Abu Ub
# Ibn Al-J

GW01425239

## The soldier of Islam and Guardian of the Ummah.

*Sara Saleem*

Ta Ha Publishers Ltd.
1 Wynne Road,
London SW9 0BB U.K.

Copyright © Ta-Ha Publishers Ltd. 1419AH / 1999CE

Reprint July 2002

Published by:
Ta-Ha Publishers Ltd.
1 Wynne Road
London SW9 0BB

Website: http://www.taha.co.uk
Email: sales@taha.co.uk

Adapted from the Arabic by: Sara Saleem
General Editor: Afsar Siddiqui

A catalogue record of this book is available from the British Library.

ISBN 0907461 43 3

Printed and bound by: Deluxe Printers, London.
email: de-luxe@Talk21.com

B'ismillah ar-Rahman ar-Raheem

# ABU UBAIDAH IBN AL-JARRAH

Chapter One.

It was a warm, balmy night in Makkah and four groups made up of the chiefs of the Qureish were sitting outside the Ka'bah talking and passing the time in their usual way. On this particular occasion, however, they had been joined by the chiefs of various other tribes who were visiting the city. The conversation focused on an event taking place in the city which was quite new and shocking to them, which occupied their thoughts totally and was difficult indeed to ignore.

One of the four chiefs of the Qureish started complaining:

"The case of Muhammad, son of Abdullah is strange indeed . . . He used to be such a sensible, intelligent boy. Now I honestly do not know what has got into him — after forty years of having lived among us he suddenly comes forth proclaiming a new

1

religion, trying to replace the religion of our fathers and grandfathers!"

"It appears to me," said another, "that the sun has finally gone to his head. But I shouldn't think that it will last for long, so don't tire yourselves out worrying about him so much."

"Especially as he is poor and alone — no-one belives in his message except his wife Khadija and his cousin, Ali. Those are the only two people in the world who believe in him and his new message."

"The message of Muhammad will reach the furthest corners of the world", joked another chief. "What, with a woman and a small boy already believing in it". The others roared with laughter.

At this moment, a young man came rushing towards them and sat down at the feet of one of the chiefs of Qureish. As he whispered in the chiefs ear, his face blackened with anger and he turned towards the others in the group.

"Woe betide Ibn Abi Qahaafa", he said.

"Who? — Abu Bakr?"

"Yes!"

"What has he done?"

"That turncoat has gone to Muhammad and become one of his helpers, that's what he's done."

"Why are you so worried about Muhammad", said another of the chiefs trying to calm him down. "And tell me, who is Muhammad to frighten us, the leaders of the tribes . . . let's forget about him. We will talk about something more useful and interesting."

* * * * *

Abu Bakr, a prominent member of Makkan society was therefore one of the earliest people to respond to the message of Islam and was also active in spreading its message. He would go in particular, in those early days to the friends whom he knew in his days of ignorance, and who he knew to possess intelligence and high moral standards. He would go in total sincerity and goodwill, and amongst those whom he helped to guide to the religion of Allah in

3

those days were 'Uthman ibn 'Affan, Sa'ad ibn Abi Waqaas and 'Abdur Rahman ibn Auf.'

One day Abu Bakr was sitting wondering which of his acquaintances of pure heart and sober mind would be willing to listen to the message of Truth — Islam. His old friend Abu Ubaida came to mind and Abu Bakr made up his mind there and then that he would go and speak with him.

The following afternoon therefore, when Abu Bakr sat and talked with his friend, the latter found his words to be quite unusual and astonishing. For one thing, they did not contain any confusing aspects or ambiguity. Still, Abu Ubaida thought it wise to proceed slowly in responding to Abu Bakr's words — he wanted to give the matter some serious thought first. So he told Abu Bakr to come back again the next day. Throughout the night Abu Ubaida thought about the invitation to Islam which his friend had extended to him. He compared it with the worshipping of idols and statues which he saw around him — and thought that this surely was not what the Creator wanted from his servants. Slowly Abu Ubaida's

heart began to fill with the Light of Islam and he became aware of the strangeness of the life which surrounded him.

Abu Bakr came to see him the next day and called out:

"Hey, Abu Ubaida, has your heart and mind been guided to the Truth?"

"Yes," came the reply "Lets go together to your companion, Muhammad, for verily his is the call to Truth".

Abu Ubaida went to the Prophet and proclaimed his submission to Islam in front of him by reciting the Shahada and promised to work for and in defence of Islam.

The Prophet's heart was gladdened by Abu Ubaida's acceptance of Islam especially as he admired his youthful vigour and qualities of leadership.

Abu Ubaida was only the eighth person to submit to Islam — apart from these few, there were no other Muslims on the face of the earth. As one of the earliest Muslims, Abu Ubaida spent most of his time in the company of the Prophet. He was a man of utmost sincerity and during this period he learnt a great deal about the Message of the Prophet and increased his Faith manifold.

Soon after Abu Ubaida's submission, the Prophet, through the Divine revelation received the order to proclaim the Message publicly. Up to this stage, the Prophet had been preaching only privately. Now he was told to proclaim out loud the Unity of Allah and to call the people to the Message of Islam in the clear light of day. The Prophet of Allah (Peace be upon him) set about to comply with this order straight away and began calling people to Islam and to his message.

The Qureish however did not want to listen at all and they closed their ears to his words. They also discouraged other men from listening to the Prophet and began to take steps towards stopping the Message of the Prophet from taking flight. They wanted to win a victory for their false gods and to smash the new religion of Muhammad which was threatening their own.

Now, these early days of spreading the Message were very dark and gloomy for the followers of the Prophet. Indeed, they faced great trials and hardships. Those earliest days have in fact been described as the most difficult of times for the Muslims. The trials, however, far from weakening the faith of the Muslims, made it stronger than ever. They stood firm as the mountains themselves against the miseries of the time. However unpleasant the unfriendly winds that blew around them, this small band of God-fearing Muslims stood solidly against them, like strong, lofty mountains.

Because of their situation, the Muslims wished dearly to be able to defend themselves and to wage a Holy War against the disbelievers. The order permitting them to wage, however, had not yet been revealed from Allah to Muhammad (p.b.u.h). It was out of the question that Muhammad would do something which had not been permitted by his Creator therefore the wisest advice he could offer them was that they emigrate to a country where they could be safe. They would merely be travelling from one piece of Allah's earth to another and would be able to practice their religion in peace and safety.

Muhammad therefore told his companions to emigrate to the land of Abyssinia which was at that time ruled by a Christian King. He told them that they would be perfectly safe in this land as the king was known for his fairness and he never oppressed anyone. Many of the Prophet's companions therefore emmigrated to Abyssinia including Uthman ibn Affan and his wife Ruqqaya, Abdur Rahman ibn Auf and Abu Ubaida ibn Jarrah.

This did not by any means mark the end of their troubles however. The Qureish chiefs sent an emmissary, Amr ibn al-Aas to follow them and to tell the King of Abyssinia, whose name was Al-Najashi, to send the companions of Muhammad back to Makkah. But the fair-minded king listened to the companions side of the story and was deeply moved to hear them recite verses from the Holy Quran recounting the birth of the Prophet Jesus (A.S.). He refused to send them back to the persecution in Makkah, and offered them refuge in his country.

Meanwhile in Makkah itself, the Message was gaining in strength and attracting more and more followers every day. At the same time, the Qureish were increasing their persecution and downright oppression of the Muslims day by day. Many of the followers of the Prophet in these early days were the poor and oppressed and they withstood magnificently the attacks of the unbelievers armed with strong belief in their hearts.

After having struggled in Makkah for thirteen years however, the Prophet began to feel that maybe this was not the most suitable place for spreading the Divine Message. He received the order from Allah to emigrate and followed his companions to Madina, a city where the atmosphere was more friendly and the people more willing to accept the Message.

In Abyssinia, the companions of the Prophet, heard about the emigration of the Messenger to Madina where they had found their brothers and helpers. The Muslims in Abyssinia, Abu Ubaida included, returned as hastily as they could to Madina so that they could at last put themselves under the leadership of the Beloved Prophet. Abu Ubaida was overjoyed to be with the Prophet again, and the Muslims felt fortunate to have a man of Abu Ubaida's

stature to be with them at this second
decisive stage in their struggle. A stage of
great effort, toil and finally expansion.

Chapter Two.

It was in the city of Madina that Muhammad received the Permission from Allah to engage in battle against those who disbelieved and fought against Islam. The Qureish, who were the Muslims greatest enemies, descended on Madina with their horses and men altogether hoping to inflict upon Muhammad and his followers a decisive defeat from which they hoped the Muslims would never recover. There followed the Battle of Badr. The two armies stood facing each other, on one side, the soldiers of Islam, and on the other side, the soldiers of Falsehood and of the accursed Shaytan. The divide between the two armies was indeed enormous.

The army of the Prophet consisted only of 313 men and camels and horses. The army of the Qureish on the other hand was made up of around 2,000 soldiers with 600 coats of armour, one hundred horses and 700 camels.

The two armies stood facing each other preparing for the decisive battle which lay ahead of them.

The Prophet passed in front of his army in order to inspect it for the last time before the battle. As he passed by Sawad ibn Ghaziya he saw that he was standing out of line with the rest, so he prodded him lightly in the stomach with his stick and said, "Straighten up this line O Sawad".

Sawad replied, "O Prophet of Allah, you have hurt me, and you have been sent with the Truth and Justice from Allah, and yet you hit me with your stick". On hearing Sawad's complaint, the Prophet did not become angry as any other Military commander, then or today would, but instead he uncovered his stomach and told Sawad to hit him. Sawad, of course, could not bring himself to hit the Just and Noble Prophet and embraced him instead.

"What made you do that?" the Prophet asked.

Sawad repiled:
"I wanted my last memory of you to be that of my skin touching yours", Sawad's words

showed how prepared he was to meet his death in that battle and how much he loved the Prophet. The Prophet wished him well.

The moment arrived for the battle to begin and the two armies engaged in deadly combat. The army of the believers displayed such heroism and a spirit of sacrifice that they served as an inspiration for Muslims for generations to come. Umair ibn al-Haman for example was listening to the Holy Prophet saying "Rise to go to Paradise, the width of which encompasses the heavens and the earth."

Umair said astonished;

"The width of the heavens and the earth?" he asked.

The Prophet replied, "Yes".

"O, excellent" replied Umair.

"What makes you say that?" asked the Prophet.

"O, I only wish that I could be one of its inhabitants".

"You are indeed of its inhabitants" replied the Prophet.

Umair produced some dates he had brought with him to sustain him throughout the battle but now he observed himself with astonishment and said:

"If I stay alive long enough to eat these dates it will be a very long life indeed."

He tossed away his dates and hurried into the thick of the battle brandishing his sword and chanting to himself words of encourgement in battle. On the battlefield he dealt a devastating blow to the enemy until he fell as a martyr in the way of Allah.

Al Auf ibn al Harith said to the Messenger of Allah;

"O Messenger of Allah, what acts of His slave does it please the Creator to see?"

The Prophet replied, "When he plunges his bare arm into the enemy".

Al-Harith took off the protective armour which he had been wearing, tossed it aside and went into the fight, killing the idol-worshippers until he himself was killed in battle.

It was Abu Ubaida however who set one of

the proudest examples at the Battle of Badr. His was a living, pulsating picture of deep faith — and of a heart that was full of courage and strength.

The belief in his heart was so pure and beautiful that it did not fear anything except Allah. Abu Ubaida was like a melody of the Qu'ran when it is beautifully recited and captivates the hearts of everyone — and makes them forget everything in existence and remember only Allah, the Creator of the heavens and the earth.

On the day of Badr, Abu Ubaida was confronted by his hostile father, Abdullah ibn Al-Jarrah who was one of the disbelievers. He was in fact determined to kill his son who had turned away from his religion of idol worship.

Abdullah ibn al Jarrah was a tall brave man and a bold horseman and he had made up his mind to kill his son on their first encounter. He would teach him a lesson for disobeying his parents, for daring to oppose his father. He faced his son and attempted to kill him but his son moved away and averted his sword from him. He moved on to another group and fought against it. The two men became seperated.

The father kept looking for his son until he caught up with him once more. He lifted his sword high and aimed a direct blow at his son. Abu Ubaida however stopped the blow with a light movement and made the sword fall to the ground. Abu Ubaida turned away once again from his father and moved as far away as he could. The two were again separated.

But the father was determined that his son should not escape him whatever it cost him. He searched for his son amidst the chaos until he caught up with him a third time. He lifted his sword high to deal his son the deadly blow which he hoped would soothe his wounded heart and calm his restless soul.

Abu Ubaida saw now that his father was intent on opposing and antagonising him and he saw in his hostility, a hostility towards Islam. Now Abu Ubaida considered himself as nothing but a soldier of Islam and therefore his father's opposition towards him was a barrier between himself and the establishment of their religion of Allah. It would prevent him from spreading the Word of Allah on His earth. Could Abu Ubaida remain silent then in the face of this kind of opposition?

No — this could not be. He had to carry out his duty towards his father. He had turned away twice already, but his father still desired to kill him. But this time it was Abu Ubaida who preceded his father in desiring to kill him.

The two swords met in combat . . .

The two men faced each other . . .

The adversaries stopped.

Beautiful memories began to stir in Abu Ubaida's mind. Sweet memories of his childhood when his father used to carry him, laughing and playing. Abu Ubaida forced himself to brush these memories aside — he would not let these memories come in the way of spreading the message of Islam and proclaiming the Word of Allah.

Abu Ubaida raised his sword — high and trembling — and dropped the sharp blade on the chest of his father, a father whose

17

heart was full of hatred and anger against Islam . . . The sword pierced his father's heart and the blood gushed forth and formed lines on the earth — painting a picture of the most beautiful sacrifice, and of great courage and bravery.

It was one of the decisive moments of Islamic history, when the sky shook and the angels recorded it on everlasting pages. The angel Gibreel revealed to the Prophet the verses;

"You will not find a peoples who believe in Allah and the Day of Judgement befriending those who have turned away from Allah and His Prophet. Even if they be their fathers or sons or relatives; these are the people who have Faith written in their hearts and who have been strengthened with a spirit from Him. he will make them enter gardens with rivers flowing underneath to live therein eternally. Allah is well pleased with them and they are pleased with Him. These are of the Party of Allah; indeed those of the Party of Allah are successful."

When Abu Ubaida heard these verses, his pained heart was soothed and his soul gladdened that Allah was pleased with him and that he was one of the Party of the Successful.

## The Conquerer of Greater Syria.

Abu Ubaida took part in all the battles in the company of the Prophet which the Muslims waged in the early days of Islam. After the death of the Prophet (Peace be upon him), Abu Ubaida continued his work as a talented military leader.

The story of the conquest of Greater Syria (which was much larger than present day Syria) is also one of great heroism and sacrifice. it bears witness to the fact that the Muslims, however small their number, were able because of their deep faith, unity and discipline, to defeat all those who stood in their way, whatever their size or number.

The conquest of Greater Syria began in the time of Abu Bakr's 'Khilafat' or rule. Abu Bakr had succeeded the Prophet as ruler of the Muslims after the Prophet's death. It was Abu Bakr's greatest desire that the Muslims should liberate Syria from Byzantine oppression

19

and bring to its people the teachings of Islam. He therefore made an appeal for the people to come forward for the Holy War and later ordered a general conscription. People came hurrying from every direction until the army had reached gigantic proportions. Abu Bakr decided however not to send the army in only one direction, but to section it into four contingents. At the head of the first section he appointed Yazid ibn Abi Sufyan and sent him at the head of his army to East Jordan. the second army he sent to Albaqa with Sharhabil at its head and third army was sent to Palestine with Amr ibn al-Aas in command. The fourth army under Abu Ubaida ibn al Jarrahwas sent to the city of Hims. Abu Ubaida was also entrusted with the overall general command of the four armies.

The Muslim armies set forth in the Name of Allah after each commander had received the following inspiring advice from the Khalifa Abu Bakr.

"When you travel, do not impose restrictions on yourself or your companions, and consult them and take their advice on matters, and be just. Keep away from oppression and tyranny. A people who are oppressive will not be successful nor will they be victorious against their enemies. When you come across the enemy do not turn your backs and flee, . . . whoever does so has brought about the anger of Allah and his refuge is hell and a miserable outcome. If you are victorious over your enemies, do not kill children or old men or women or babies. Do not wound (anything) except livestock for eating. Do not deceive once you have made a contract or violate a treaty once you have made peace."

Abu Ubaida now passed by various towns and valleys on his way to Hims. When he finally reached Hims, his army laid siege to it until it was forced to open its arms to admit the conquering, successful army.

Then it was that the Byzantians decided to unleash their full fury and prepared their armies to block the success of the conquering armies which had burst forth from the Arabian peninsula. This time their army totalled 240,000 soldiers.

Abu Ubaida recognised the grave danger his army was in, composed as it was of hardly more than 80,000 soldiers. He sent a message to Abu Bakr, informing him of the dangerous situation. Abu Bakr sent him some reinforcements but Abu Ubaida realised that these even would not be sufficient. He saw as the only answer the joining of all four Muslim armies, only together they would be able to beat back the Byzantine army. Abu Ubaida therefore sent messages to the leaders of the three other armies explaining to them the situation which his army was facing and advising them to act accordingly. The three Muslim commanders wrote to Abu Bakr informing him also of the grave situation and asking for his opinion and advice.

Abu Bakr wrote back telling the Commanders to join forces and form one unified army to repulse the idolators.

"You are the helpers of Allah" he told them, "and Allah helps those who help Him and not those who disbelieve in Him. People such as you will not be weakened by any deficiency, but whoever is faced with sinfulness, let him be wary of it. Let every man amongst you unite with his companion." Then he added, "May Allah divert the helpers from the whisperings of the devil with the help of Khalid ibn Walid."

\* \* \* \* \*

Abu Bakr sent for Khalid, who was at the time in Iraq, and who was one of the most famous soldiers and military commanders of Islam. Khalid was ordered to go to Syria to take command of the united Islamic army and to bring with him half of his army to aid that of Abu Ubaida, and to leave the other half in Iraq under the command of Muthanna ibn Haritha as-Shaybani.

And Abu Bakr sent a letter to Abu Ubaida:

In the Name of Allah the Most Beneficiant and Most Merciful.

From Abdullah ibn Ateeq ibn Abi Qahafa to Abi Ubaida ibn al Jarrah, May the peace of Allah be upon you.

I have entrusted Khalid with the task of routing the enemy in Syria — do not oppose him therefore — and listen well to him and obey him, I have given him authority over you. I know that you are better than him but

I felt that he has a better understanding of war which you do not have — May Allah guide us and protect us and yourself to the straight path.

Khalid ibn Walid also wrote to Abi Ubaida from Iraq.

His letter went thus:

In the Name of Allah the Most Beneficiant and Most Merciful

From Khalid ibn Walid to Abi Ubaida ibn al-Jarrah.

May the peace of Allah be upon you I have received a letter from the Successor (khalifa) of the Messenger of Allah which orders me to travel to Syria and to take charge of the soldiers there and take responsibility for their situation. By Allah I did not ask for this responsibility nor did I want it — you are now in the position in which I was in — we will not disobey or contradict you. Nor will we do anything against your order. You are the leader of the Muslims, we do not deny your virtue but think of you as indispensable.

How evident in these letters is the sincerity

and brotherhood of the early Muslim commanders and leaders, their humility and deep faith.

So Khalid arrived in Syria and the Islamic armies gathered together joined by his force of 10,000. At last the Islamic and Byzantian armies faced each other across the valley of Yarmuk. The Muslims were by far outnumbered by the enemy who also had eight thousand horses.

Abu Ubaida stood to make an appeal to the Muslims.

"O servants of Allah: help Allah and He will help you and will strengthen you O community of Muslims: Have patience for Patience safeguards against disbelief and is pleasing to Allah and keeps away dishonour. Do not leave your lines, and do not step towards them or be the first to start the killing. Do not point your arrows at them or shield yourselves with your shields — keep silent except to remember Allah, most Exalted within yourselves until the matter is settled by the Grace of Allah.

The two armies met in battle. The fighting was very fierce, more intense than anything the Muslims had engaged in before. Often throughout the battle the old companions of the Holy Prophet would stop fighting to encourage the Muslims and remind them of the Message of Allah and of His Prophet and give them the good tidings of the Help of Allah which was close at hand.

Amr ibn al-Aas stood in the middle of his army and said:

O Muslims . . .

I have heard that the Muslims will conquer this land village by village and castle by castle so do not let their size or their number terrify you. If you prove to be true however, you will scatter them like pigeons.

Abu Sufyan said;

O Muslims,

Be prepared for what lies ahead — infront of you is the Prophet of Allah and Paradise and behind you is the devil and the Fire.

Abu Huraira said;

"Hurry to the delights of the Paradise and to

26

your Lord, the Exalted and Magnificient in luxurious gardens . . .

As the battle raged on, and men fell on both sides, dead and wounded, one of the Muslims said to Khalid ibn Walid,

"There are so many Byzantians compared to us Muslims"

"Shame on you" replied Khalid, "Are you trying to make me afraid of the Byzantines? . . . How I wish my horse Al-Ashqar had recovered from his affliction and that they were doubled in number".

During the battle a man from among the enemy ranks who was called Mahan came looking for Khalid and requested to be allowed to see him to talk on some important matter. He was granted the request and when Khalid appeared he said to him,

"We have heard that you people have only come out from the land of the Arabs because you were driven by great hunger — so how about if we give each man among you ten dinars (the Arab form of money) and a garment and food — will you return to your country? Then again next year we will send you the same again."

Khalid told him;

"We were not forced out of our country for this reason — we are a people who drink blood," he joked, "and we had heard that the blood of the Byzantians is the very best so we came here for that reason."

Mahan left, truly astonished.

The battle grew even fiercer — iron clashed with iron and might with might.

Akrama ibn Abi Jahl called out to his fellow Muslims;

"Who will make a contract with death?"

His uncle alHarith ibn Hashim made the contract with him and so did Darar ibn alAzwar and others — the number in fact reached four hundred — then they burst forth on the Byzantians leading the way with their swords, tearing them apart with their faith until many of them met their Lord happy and content. Darar was amongst them.

During the battle, Abu Ubaida received a letter from Madina, which was the capital of the Islamic world, saying that the Khalifa

Abu Bakr al Siddiq had passed away and had been succeeded by Umar ibn Al-Khattab. The letter was infact from Umar telling him that Khalid ibn Walid should be relieved of his position as commander of the army and replaced by Abu Ubaida.

Abu Ubaida folded the letter and put it in his pocket. He did not want to inform Khalid of this order until after the battle had finished. The Muslims continued their brave, fearless battle against the Byzantines until they succeeded in inflicting a crushing defeat . . .

The muezzin announced that the victory was of the Muslims.

Abu Ubaida now took over the leadership from Khalid and wrote to Umar asking him what his next assignment would be. Umar ordered him to go to Damascus because it was the fortress of Syria and the seat of the King. Abu Ubaida prepared his army and set off for Damascus. On the way his army encountered the Byzantians again and a fierce battle ensued which the Muslims won.

The army then laid seige to the city of

Damascus, surrounding it for well on six whole months after which its inhabitants surrendered and made a contract with Abu Ubaida. He spent some time sorting out the affairs of the city and then made the journey to Hims. His army also succeeded in opening the doors of this city with the help of Allah and sent back the good news in a letter to Umar. From there the army went north to capture Hama, Aleppo and many other Syrian cities, until indeed the entire surface of Syria had been placed under the glorious flag of Islam.

* * * * *

## Some of the virtues of Abu Ubaida.

Abu Ubaida, was one of the very first people to have accepted Islam, as we have mentioned. During his lifetime, he was one of the people to have been given the good tidings of heaven from the Prophet of Allah — one of the ten people to have received this news from the Prophet. His life had been one full of firm, sincere faith and of a rare heroism, as well as acts of virtue and noble behaviour.

## The Wish.

Umar ibn al-Khattab was sitting amongst a group of his companions, talking about certain affairs of state. When the business had finished Umar, peace be upon him, looked at them for a long time, examining their faces. At last he said;

"Make a wish."

The group was silent for a short while, thinking about what answer they should give. A man from amongst them broke the silence and said;

"I wish that this place was full of gold so that I could spend it in the way of Allah, the Exalted and Magnificent."

But it appeared that this reply did not please Umar very much, and he said to them again;

"Make a wish."

Now another man said;

"I wish that this place was full of pearls,

31

crystals and jewels so that I could spend it in the way of Allah and give it away as charity."

Umar again shook his head and said;

"Again make a wish."

This time the companions were really astonished and said to Umar, may Allah be pleased with him;

"We do not know how we should reply to you, O Commander of the Faithful."

Umar smiled and said;

"I wish that it were full of men such as Abu Ubaida ibn al. Jarrah."

What did Umar mean by his reply?"

The other companions had wished that Allah would fill the house they were in with riches so that they could spend it in His way. But Umar alone had the truest understanding of the value of courageous men and therefore his wish had been for such men and not riches. Riches could not spread the Message of Allah or establish the philosophy of Islam as well as people with deep faith could. The religion propagated by men of true faith would be durable and everlasting and thus Umar had made his wish for such men, rather than money. Men of the calibre of Abu Ubaida ibn al-Jarrah. men of rare courage and pure belief who could fill this world with light and raise the banner of Islam in the four corners of the earth . . .

## The Ascetic.

Abu Ubaida was a man who of his own accord forsook the vanities, the material benefits of this world. He chose not to take pleasure in worldly delights, desiring nothing except closeness with his Lord and Creator . . . for the Pleasure of Allah, as every Muslim knows, is better and everlasting.

The life of Abu Ubaida was an exemplary one, the life which every Muslim would benefit from knowing about. He was a man who had a total control of his own self, control over his desires and wishes. It has been related of Umar ibn al-Khattab that when he went forward to open the Sacred mosque he was met by army commanders and the greatest leaders of the city (of Jerusalem). Umar asked, "Where is my brother?"

The commanders asked him who he meant. Umar replied, "Abu Ubaida ibn al-Jarrah.

They said, "He is just coming now."

Abu Ubaida arrived on a camel and Umar greeted him and told the other people to leave them. Umar went with Abu Ubaida until he arrived at the place where Abu Ubaida was staying.

Umar asked, "Where is your furniture and belongings, O Abu Ubaida?"

All he could see in the house was his sword and a horse. He also asked him where the food was. Abu Ubaida produced some slices of bread, a bowl and a waterskin. He brought forward some nuts. This was the only food in his house. Umar was visibly upset and said to Abu Ubaida, "If only you would make your house more comfortable for yourself."

But Abu Ubaida replied, "O Commander of the Faithful, we will have all those comforts later." (By which he meant in the life after death).

Umar said to him, "You have changed our world, we are all envious of you, O Abu Ubaida."

Thus Abu Ubaida found consolation in following the leadership of the Prophet (peace be upon him) and remembered the noble hadith, "Nothing is more fearful for you than the fleeting enjoyments of this world — that which is with Allah is better and everlasting."

Abu Ubaida continued to the end of his earthly days living in the utmost simplicity and humility. He died having carried out the recommendation given by the Holy Prophet to his companions. "Those of you who are most dear to me and the closest to me are those who will meet me (in the next world) in the same state in which you left me."

* * * * *

As well as being an ascetic in the life of this world, Abu Ubaida was also a man who feared Allah, the Exalted and Magnificient, and would often cry while he was praying and would implore Allah in humility. He was really a very modest man — arrogance had no place in his heart whatsoever.

Abu Hadifa has written the following story on the conquest of Syria.

While he was in Syria, Abu Ubaida received a message from the Byzantines saying that they wanted to send an emmissary to propose a peace plan. They said;

"If you accept then surely it will be best for you and for us. But if you refuse we will wish you only harm."

They were told to send whoever they wanted. They sent a tall man with red hair and blue eyes. When he arrived he stood amongst the Muslims and asked to be shown to the leader, Abu Ubaida.

"Here he is", they replied. The man looked around and saw Abu Ubaida sitting down, holding the reigns of his horse in one hand, and some arrows in the other hand.

"You are the leader?" he asked Abu Ubaida.

Abu Ubaida replied that he was.

"Why are you sitting on the ground?" he asked "Will sitting on a cushion or a carpet humble you in the sight of Allah — or will it stop you from performing good deeds?"

Abu Ubaida replied that Allah does not shy away from the reality — "Yesterday I was in need of some provisions so I borrowed from this brother of mine — Ma'az ibn Jabl. We are the servants of Allah" he said, "we walk on the earth, we eat on the earth and we sit on the earth, that does not lessen us in the eyes of Allah; rather our rewards are magnified by these acts and our position is elevated. Now continue and say what you came to say."

Such was the humility of Abu Ubaida — the humility of a true believer which elevates him in the eyes of Allah by many degrees.

## The Plague

The days went by quickly. Abu Ubaida was

still in Syria in the year 18 A.H. (After Hijra) with his soldiers working to establish the Glory of Allah on the earth. Now in this same year, an outbreak of the plague occurred in the town of 'Amwaas where troops of Abu Ubaida were positioned.

The plague was very severe and many, many Muslims, an estimated 30,000 died.

The plague in fact is a very old illness which many doctors have said originated in India and China from where it spread over the entire earth. It was a most obnoxious malady which decimated whole populations, not sparing anyone in its path. Perhaps you have heard about the plague of Europe of the fourteenth century C.E. which caused the death of some 20 million people. People have differed as to the causes of the plague. Some say that it is a manifestation of the anger of Allah, the Exalted, on the people who have done wrong and evil. Some say that it is the work of the devil and others that it comes from accumulations of festering rubbish.

In Europe in the dark middle ages, the people said that the Plague was the work of

the Jews and they therefore began to oppress the Jews severely. They herded them into clusters and groups, put them in wooden huts and set fire to them.

Umar, the Khalifa, May Peace be upon him, felt concerned about Abu Ubaida who was at risk from the plague in Syria and devised a plan to get him out of there, before he also was struck down. He decided on sending him a letter which said:

"I have need of you here. No one else can do. I am more determined than you, if you receive my letter at night do not wait for morning before you start to make your way towards me. If you receive it in the daytime, then do not wait until the evening before you make your way here."

Abu Ubaida read Umar's letter. He understood the real intention behind the letter of the Commander of the Faithful and replied thus:

"I have recognised your need for me, O Commander of the Faithful. Please excuse me from fulfilling this request of yours. I am but a soldier amongst the Muslim soldiers, I do not want to be anything different from them."

When Umar read the letter, he cried and the tears gushed down his cheeks.

The plague spread over Syria until it covered a quarter of the entire country. And Abu Ubaida himself inevitably became ill with the plague. One of his companions, 'Arbad ibn Sariya went to see him and related to him that he had heard that the Prophet of Allah, (Peace be upon him) had said that the person who dies of the plague is a martyr; and the person who dies of an intestinal ailment is a martyr; and a person who is drowned is a martyr; and a person who dies from burning is a martyr.

The illness became more severe and Abu Ubaida called his commanders and gave them his famous advice and he told them to bury him wherever he died.

In the year 18 A.H. Abu Ubaida passed away at the age of fifty-four years. He was buried in the Jordan valley.

The Prophet of Allah (Peace be upon him) has said;

"Every nation has a guardian, and the guardian of this nation is Abu Ubaida ibn al-Jarrah."

THE
MUSLIM EMPIRE
ca. 750
English Miles
0    200   400   600

Conquests under the Prophet and first Caliph, 622-634
   "    "   the second and third Caliphs, 634-656
   "    "   the Umayyads to al-Walid I, 681-715
Sulaymān, 715-717, and his successors to 750

FARGHĀNAH
TUKHĀRISTĀN
Samarqand
Bukhārā
Balkh
Kābul
Multan
SIND
Indus R.
KHWĀRIZM
Marw
KHURĀSĀN
PERSIA
Nihāwand
AL-JIBAL
Baghdād
Samarra
AL-'IRĀQ
FĀRIS
Iṣṭakhr
Shīrāz
KARMĀN
MUKRĀN
'UMĀN
Al-Daybul
CASPIAN SEA
ARMENIA
Al-Mawṣil
AL-JAZĪRAH
Tigris R.
Euphrates R.
Al-Kūfah
Al-Ḥīrah
AL-BASRAH
Al-Baṣrah
Edessa
Jerusalem
SYRIA
PERSIAN GULF
ARABIA
NAJD
AL-YAMAN
AL-ḤIJĀZ
Medina
Mecca
ḤAḌRAMAWT
Nazwā
RED SEA
BLACK SEA
BULGARS
Constantinople
Abydos
Brusa
Sardis
Qūniyah
EASTERN ROMAN EMPIRE
CILICIA
Tarsus
Cyprus
AEGEAN SEA
Rome
EASTERN MEDITERRANEAN SEA
IFRĪQIYAH
Al-Qayrawān
Barqah
EGYPT
Al-Fusṭāṭ
Nile R.
NUBIA
FRANCE
ASTURIAS
ANDALUSIA
Toledo
Cordova
Tangier
AL-MAGHRIB